"Without leaps of imagination, or dreaming, we lose the excitement of possibilities. Dreaming, after all, is a form of planning."

~Gloria Steinem

"I Am Enough" Workbook

A Guidebook and Journal for Building Personal Power and Seizing Opportunities

by Danielle Palli

Cover Art: Elizabeth Von Hohen Brosha

Copyright © 2022 Danielle Palli

All rights reserved. No part of the publication may be reproduced or transmitted in any form or by any means, electronic, mechanical, photocopying, or recording for any information storage or retrieval systems, without written permission from the publisher.

Request for permission to make copies of any part of the work should write to: Danielle@birdlandmediaworks.com

Published by Birdland Media Works 2022

Library of Congress Cataloging-in-publication Data
Palli, Danielle (author)

The "I Am Enough" Workbook/ Danielle Palli

ISBN: 978-1-7367982-2-5
Printed in the USA
First Edition

This book is to be used for personal growth and is not intended as a replacement for therapy or medical advice.

Table of Contents:

How to Use This Guidebook 5
What Does Emotional Well-being Mean to Me? 6
Artful Listening 10
Breathing Into Stress 14
Write Your Own Affirmation 18
Pennies from Heaven 22
Draw Your Emotional Landscape 26
Gathering Your Tribe 30
Watching Yourself on a Movie Screen 34
3 Miracles a Day 38
The Power of Play 42
From Victim to Victor 46
Creating Your Perfect Day 50
Self-Reflection 54
Sounds of Silence 58
What if You Never Met 62
Become an Emotional Alchemist 66
Spreading the Joy 70
"I Am Not My Thoughts" 74
Creating Your Personal Symbol 78
My Award 80
The Path Not Taken 82
Digging Into Your Strengths 86
Intuitive Eating 90
"This is a Disaster!" 93
Forest Bathing & More 96
Draw Your Superhero Uniform 99

Become a RAK-tivist 102
Noticing the Good 106
Discovering Your Values 110
Problem-Solving Strategies 114
Impossible Solutions 118
Going With Your Gut 120
Finding the Value 124
Gifts to the World 128
Discovering a Power Animal 132
Walking Meditation 136
Telling a Different Story 140
Super Powers & Kryptonite 144
Giving Up Control 148
"I Can Do It Myself!" 152
Time After Time 156
To Know Me Is to Love Me 160
A New Perspective 164
Silencing the Inner Critic 168
Passive, Aggressive ... Just Right 172
Right Now, Later, Never 176
What's Your Vision Statement? 180
3 Wishes Come True 182
My Future's So Bright 186
Go Forth and Be Musical! 190
Freestyle 192
Freestyle 196

How to Use This Guidebook

Welcome! I'm so happy you're here.

I created the **"I Am Enough" Guidebook** as a resource for anyone who could use a little daily positivity and support throughout the week. If you're seeking tools for building personal power, finding what brings you meaning and purpose, developing greater self-awareness, creating better relationships, and inviting more joy into your life, you have come to the right place.

As a Board-Certified Positive Psychology Health and Wellness Coach and a Mindfulness Coach, I've integrated my background in emotional intelligence, positive psychology, cognitive behavior theory, and a variety of spiritual and holistic modalities together to create the workbook that I wished someone had given me several decades ago.

Each week, you are invited to complete one activity which may include journaling, drawing or some other form of creative expression. Then, you will be asked to work with that concept every day for the remainder of the week and record how you are feeling and, when applicable, what your observations were about yourself and the experience. (e.g., If you start on Monday, then your daily log will be from Tuesday through Sunday.)

There are 50 activities that you can choose to do in any order, with two "freestyle" weeks where you can choose to repeat any of the previous activities that you particularly enjoyed. **NOTE: There are minor variations to the format for select weeks.**

I hope that this guidebook leaves you happier, more inspired, and with a greater sense of your own awesome power.

Well-Being Weekly Check-In
How are you feeling today? (Circle one)

What Does Emotional Well-being Mean to Me?
Discovering What Brings You Peace

What makes our life meaningful, purposeful, happy, and fulfilling is different for each person. For some, emotional well-being might include having a large family and a large social circle. For others, it might be plenty of alone time in the forest and a healthy balance between career and downtime. As you consider all the aspects of your life, such as your health, finances, relationships, career, and so forth, reflect on what it means to live a balanced life and enjoy emotional well-being.

On the next page, draw, create a collage, write words all over the page, or in some way depict your vision of emotional well-being. Throughout the remainder of the week, use the spaces provided to jot down ways you contribute to this well-being daily.

Creative Space

Day/Date: _____

Weekly Tracker

Day/Date: _____

Day/Date: _____

Day/Date: _____

Day/Date: _____

Day/Date: _____

Day/Date: _____

Weekly Wrap-Up

Use this space to note any final observations about this activity. What surprised you? What was challenging? What did you like or dislike about the activity? Write your summary below.

_____
_____
_____
_____
_____
_____
_____
_____
_____
_____
_____
_____
_____
_____
_____

Well-Being Weekly Check-In
How are you feeling today? (Circle one)

Artful Listening
Giving the Gift of Time

We live in a busy, noisy, "got to be moving all the time" world. If you've ever called someone and begun the conversation with "I'm sorry to bother you, but—" or been annoyed when a friend was taking too long to "get to the point" of a story, you know what I'm talking about. Giving the gift of time is one of the best ways to show people around you that you care about them, thereby deepening your relationships and boosting your own well-being in the process. Studies continually show us that supporting others makes us happier.

On the next page, write about an event in your life where someone gave you the gift of time by simply listening and allowing you to feel heard. How did it make you feel? Throughout the rest of the week, note moments where you practiced artful listening.

Journal Space
Day/Date: _____

Weekly Tracker

Day/Date: _____

Day/Date: _____

Day/Date: _____

Day/Date: _____

Day/Date: _____

Day/Date: _____

Weekly Wrap-Up

Use this space to note any final observations about this activity. What surprised you? What was challenging? What did you like or dislike about the activity? Write your summary below.

_____
_____
_____
_____
_____
_____
_____
_____
_____
_____
_____
_____
_____
_____
_____

Well-Being Weekly Check-In
How are you feeling today? (Circle one)

Breathing Into Stress
A Practice in Mindfulness

Studies support that people who regularly practice mindfulness are less stressed, happier, remain calmer in stressful situations, are better problem-solvers, and are more resilient to life's challenges. One way to begin a mindfulness practice is by pausing throughout the day to check in with how you are feeling emotionally and physically, and simply observing what's happening in your body and your environment. This week, the challenge is to stop what you are doing at three random times throughout each day to conduct a mindful "check-in."

For this activity, find a quiet place where you can be undisturbed for at least ten minutes (set a timer if you need to). Sit comfortably and close your eyes. Draw your awareness to your breath, simply noticing the inhalation and exhalation. If your mind wanders, draw your attention back to your breath. When you are done, jot down any observations about how you are feeling physically and emotionally and if there were specific thoughts that kept coming to mind.

Journal Space

Day/Date: _____

Weekly Tracker

Day/Date: _____

Day/Date: _____

Day/Date: _____

Day/Date: _____

Day/Date: _____

Day/Date: _____

Weekly Wrap-Up

Use this space to note any final observations about this activity. What surprised you? What was challenging? What did you like or dislike about the activity? Write your summary below.

_____
_____
_____
_____
_____
_____
_____
_____
_____
_____
_____
_____
_____
_____
_____

Well-Being Weekly Check-In
How are you feeling today? (Circle one)

Write Your Own Affirmation
Speaking Kindly to Yourself

We often say negative things to ourselves. But would you speak that way to a friend? Probably not (if you're a good friend!). Consider what a friend might say to you as encouragement in an area of your life. What if you could have that "cheerleader" with you all week? This activity involves creating your own affirmation to support you throughout the week. It can be as little or as long as you like. Examples include, "I am enough," "I am more powerful than I realize," "My day flows with grace and ease."

On the next page, list a few ways in which you could use support or motivation in multiple areas of your life. See if you can create one affirmation that's all-encompassing for each of these areas. Write and re-write variations of your affirmation, until you come up with one you like. Throughout the week, repeat the affirmation throughout the day and note how your day goes.

Journal Space

Day/Date: _____

Weekly Tracker

Day/Date: _____

Day/Date: _____

Day/Date: _____

Day/Date: _____

Day/Date: _____

Day/Date: _____

Weekly Wrap-Up

Use this space to note any final observations about this activity. What surprised you? What was challenging? What did you like or dislike about the activity? Write your summary below.

_____
_____
_____
_____
_____
_____
_____
_____
_____
_____
_____
_____
_____

Well-Being Weekly Check-In
How are you feeling today? (Circle one)

Pennies from Heaven
Spending Your Fortune

Whether you are someone who believes in sending out positive energy and manifesting abundance, or someone who simply wants to generate emotional well-being by focusing on something positive (which makes us physically and mentally healthier), try this activity for one week. Imagine you've just won a great fortune (no limit to the amount). How are you going to spend it?

In the space provided, write, draw, create a collage, or in some way document what you would do with your fortune. Over the next week, think of daily ways in which you would spend it, stopping throughout the day and considering all the ways your life would be enhanced.

Creative Space

Day/Date: _____

Weekly Tracker

Day/Date: _____

Day/Date: _____

Day/Date: _____

Day/Date: _____

Day/Date: _____

Day/Date: _____

Weekly Wrap-Up

Use this space to note any final observations about this activity. What surprised you? What was challenging? What did you like or dislike about the activity? Write your summary below.

_____

_____

_____

_____

_____

_____

_____

_____

_____

_____

_____

_____

_____

_____

_____

Well-Being Weekly Check-In
How are you feeling today? (Circle one)

Draw Your Emotional Landscape
What's Going On Inside?

Sometimes, it's difficult to describe how we're feeling in words. Or, we may have trouble identifying how we are feeling on a moment-to-moment basis. This activity invites you to draw a visual representation of what's going on inside your mind and body at this moment. How you define that is up to you. For example, if you're feeling angry, perhaps you might draw a tropical storm or an abstract with lots of red and images of fire. Or, perhaps you notice butterflies in your belly and draw a visual representation of your body with butterflies fluttering in your stomach.

Take a few moments to close your eyes and take several long breaths in and out through your nose. Tune inward and notice how you are feeling emotionally and physically. When you're ready, open your eyes and draw a representation on the page provided. Throughout the week, repeat this activity on a smaller scale by drawing a symbol or thumbnail sketch of how you are feeling (or, if you prefer, jot down words to describe it).

Creative Space
Day/Date: _____

Weekly Tracker

Day/Date: _____

Day/Date: _____

Day/Date: _____

Day/Date: _____

Day/Date: _____

Day/Date: _____

Weekly Wrap-Up

Use this space to note any final observations about this activity. What surprised you? What was challenging? What did you like or dislike about the activity? Write your summary below.

_____
_____
_____
_____
_____
_____
_____
_____
_____
_____
_____
_____
_____
_____

Well-Being Weekly Check-In
How are you feeling today? (Circle one)

Gathering Your Tribe
Calling in Your Supporters

One of the best predictors of living a long and healthy life is whether or not we have a close and supportive social circle. Whether that circle is one or two close friends or family members or a large group is defined by you. Some people are naturally extroverted and social, while others prefer more alone time. Therefore, the purpose this week is for both personality types to connect with a different person each day via phone, email, video chat, or in person (not social media!). It might be reaching out to someone dear to you with whom you lost contact due to life's "busyness," or meeting up with a close friend for coffee. Ideally, in person is preferable for at least 20 minutes. But the real goal is to retain and strengthen connections.

On the next page, record who you reached out to today. How did you connect? What did you talk about? Also, note what it is about this person that you admire and why they are your friend (you might even share that information with them). Throughout the week, connect with someone new each day. Begin to notice what qualities you value in your tribe.

Journal Space

Day/Date: _____

Weekly Tracker

Day/Date: _____

Day/Date: _____

Day/Date: _____

Day/Date: _____

Day/Date: _____

Day/Date: _____

Weekly Wrap-Up

Use this space to note any final observations about this activity. What surprised you? What was challenging? What did you like or dislike about the activity? Write your summary below.

_____

_____

_____

_____

_____

_____

_____

_____

_____

_____

_____

_____

_____

_____

_____

Well-Being Weekly Check-In
How are you feeling today? (Circle one)

Watching Yourself On a Movie Screen
Expressing Yourself in a Healthy Way

Have you ever witnessed someone behaving irrationally and thought, "I wish they could see themselves as we see them right now?" This is an activity about mentally imagining yourself stepping outside of yourself and viewing your actions as an outside observer. It is not to be critical of yourself. Instead, it's about taking an honest look at how you present yourself to others and how they might perceive you.

In the space provided, write about a time in the recent past when you have had concerns about how you acted or how people perceived your actions. Perhaps it was a work disagreement or a time when you reacted in a way that was less than ideal. Except, imagine you are in the audience, watching yourself on a movie screen as you describe the event. Talk about yourself in the 3rd person. (i.e. "She reacted by ...) What do your observations reveal? What might you have done differently had you been able to see yourself?

Journal Space
Day/Date: _____

Weekly Tracker

Day/Date: _____

Day/Date: _____

Day/Date: _____

Day/Date: _____

Day/Date: _____

Day/Date: _____

Weekly Wrap-Up

Use this space to note any final observations about this activity. What surprised you? What was challenging? What did you like or dislike about the activity? Write your summary below.

_____

_____

_____

_____

_____

_____

_____

_____

_____

_____

_____

_____

_____

Well-Being Weekly Check-In
How are you feeling today? (Circle one)

3 Miracles a Day
Believing in Magic

Albert Einstein is noted for saying, "There are only two ways to live your life. One is as though nothing is a miracle. The other is as if everything is a miracle." This week is an exercise in finding miracles. You define what that is. For example, did you find the one open parking spot in a crowded lot that happens to be right in front of the store where you're heading? Or was it something big, like two rival neighbors settled their disputes and became friends? By noticing the "unbelievable" we begin to focus on the positive and develop a more optimistic view of life.

In the space provided, write down at least 3 miracles that you've witnessed within the last 24 hours. If so inclined, add what makes them a miracle and how it impacted you in a positive way. Throughout the week, document the new miracles you discover.

Journal Space

Day/Date: _____

Weekly Tracker

Day/Date: _____

Day/Date: _____

Day/Date: _____

Day/Date: _____

Day/Date: _____

Day/Date: _____

Weekly Wrap-Up

Use this space to note any final observations about this activity. What surprised you? What was challenging? What did you like or dislike about the activity? Write your summary below.

_____

_____

_____

_____

_____

_____

_____

_____

_____

_____

_____

_____

_____

_____

_____

Well-Being Weekly Check-In
How are you feeling today? (Circle one)

The Power of Play
Just for the Fun of It

As children, we were likely encouraged to "go outside and play." It was good exercise, helped us tap into our creativity, provided a healthy way to deal with stress, connected us to nature, and helped us develop friendships. But as adults, we often value productivity over play and miss out on all the benefits of play. This week, try to dedicate at least one full day to "play." Throughout the week, give yourself at least one hour a day to do something just for the fun of it. Whether it's an outdoor adventure or simply enjoying the luxury of playing a video or card game, go forth and be playful!

In the space provided, sketch a representation of what your play day entailed. Each day this week, use the spaces provided to sketch or write out what fun you had.

Creative Space

Day/Date: _____

Weekly Tracker

Day/Date: _____

Day/Date: _____

Day/Date: _____

Day/Date: _____

Day/Date: _____

Day/Date: _____

Weekly Wrap-Up

Use this space to note any final observations about this activity. What surprised you? What was challenging? What did you like or dislike about the activity? Write your summary below.

_____
_____
_____
_____
_____
_____
_____
_____
_____
_____
_____
_____
_____
_____
_____

Well-Being Weekly Check-In
How are you feeling today? (Circle one)

From Victim to Victor
Learning What's in Your Control...and What Isn't

When facing stressful situations, there is a danger in falling into one of two extreme categories: 1) Trying to control every aspect of a situation (which is impossible) or 2) Falling victim in a "Why does this always happen to me?" sort-of way. Most sages will tell you that wisdom comes from establishing what is in your control (i.e., what you can change) and taking action, and understanding what is out of your control (i.e., what you cannot change). This activity is an exercise in empowering us to control what we can and accept what we can't. With acceptance comes peace.

In the space provided, think of a recent stressful situation, perhaps one that left you feeling like a victim. Perhaps you were misunderstood or treated unfairly. Or, maybe you were a "victim" of circumstance and bad luck. In the space below, describe the situation and answer the questions: 1) What can I change in this situation? 2) What is beyond my control?

Journal Space

Day/Date: _____

Weekly Tracker

Day/Date: _____

Day/Date: _____

Day/Date: _____

Day/Date: _____

Day/Date: _____

Day/Date: _____

Weekly Wrap-Up

Use this space to note any final observations about this activity. What surprised you? What was challenging? What did you like or dislike about the activity? Write your summary below.

_____

_____

_____

_____

_____

_____

_____

_____

_____

_____

_____

_____

_____

_____

Well-Being Weekly Check-In
How are you feeling today? (Circle one)

Creating Your Perfect Day
Imagining the Best

What if you woke up one day and realized that you could do whatever you wanted because money was not a concern, you were perfectly healthy, and you had no obligations? From sun up to sun down, how would you spend that day? Perhaps you already have several days in mind, some on vacation and having fun, and others when you are contributing to the world through volunteering or work. Choose one scenario to work with. Leave room at the end to add in a few elements from "alternate" days.

In the space provided, describe your perfect day. Next, throughout the week, write down any elements from each "real" day that reflect how you would spend your "perfect" day. Are there ways to bring more of those elements into your life regularly?

Journal Space

Day/Date: _____

_____
_____
_____
_____
_____
_____
_____
_____
_____
_____
_____
_____
_____
_____
_____
_____
_____
_____
_____

Weekly Tracker

Day/Date: _____

Day/Date: _____

Day/Date: _____

Day/Date: _____

Day/Date: _____

Day/Date: _____

Weekly Wrap-Up

Use this space to note any final observations about this activity. What surprised you? What was challenging? What did you like or dislike about the activity? Write your summary below.

Well-Being Weekly Check-In

How are you feeling today? (Circle one)

Self-Reflection
Mirror, Mirror on the Wall

Many of us have a love-hate relationship with our bodies. We want to be physically capable and also attractive, and may yell at our bodies for whatever we perceive they "lack." Whether it's losses with age or injury, inabilities or just never being____[Insert your criticism here, such as "skinny" "pretty," "strong," etc.,] enough. This week, do something really scary. Take several minutes a day to simply look at yourself in the mirror, either clothed or naked.

Using only positive self-talk, describe yourself below. Then, for the remainder of the week, revisit your reflection daily and add new observations in the space provided and any positive affirmations that you find helpful (e.g., "I like the warmth of my smile," or "I have lost three pounds, and I like the way I look and feel.")

Journal Space

Day/Date: _____

Weekly Tracker

Day/Date: _____

Day/Date: _____

Day/Date: _____

Day/Date: _____

Day/Date: _____

Day/Date: _____

Weekly Wrap-Up

Use this space to note any final observations about this activity. What surprised you? What was challenging? What did you like or dislike about the activity? Write your summary below.

_____
_____
_____
_____
_____
_____
_____
_____
_____
_____
_____
_____
_____
_____

Well-Being Weekly Check-In

How are you feeling today? (Circle one)

Sounds of Silence
Quieting the Inner and Outer Chatter

When was the last time you experienced silence? The truth is, we live in a noisy world. We fight with external sounds such as traffic, people talking, music playing, and the constant exposure to electronic devices from the television to the computer, to cell phones. And we fight with our internal world, the To Do lists circulating in our minds, the self-talk and endless inner chatter. This activity is about experiencing silence. When we do so, we experience greater calm and mental clarity. Every day this week, set aside at least one hour of silence (a full day or two is better, if possible), where you shut off all electronic devices, you remain quiet and avoid conversations, and create a quiet space for yourself. This may mean telling loved ones your plan so that people understand you are in silent mode. Address the inner chatter through meditation, journaling your thoughts, drawing, or going for a walk in nature.

On the next page, draw, create a collage, write words all over the page, or in some way describe what the experience is like. For the rest of the week, reflect on your silent moments either during or immediately after the experience. How do you feel when you take a brief retreat from the world?

Creative Space

Day/Date: _____

Weekly Tracker

Day/Date: _____

Day/Date: _____

Day/Date: _____

Day/Date: _____

Day/Date: _____

Day/Date: _____

Weekly Wrap-Up

Use this space to note any final observations about this activity. What surprised you? What was challenging? What did you like or dislike about the activity? Write your summary below.

Well-Being Weekly Check-In
How are you feeling today? (Circle one)

What if You Never Met?
Appreciation for Those Around You

This week's activity is about expressing gratitude and appreciation for the people around us. Perhaps we've become so accustomed to their support that we take it (and them) for granted. Or, maybe there's a person in your life who "bugs" you sometimes, but typically, they are one of your closest friends. Or, perhaps you simply want to enhance your existing relationships. In this exercise, call to mind someone in your life who you care about. Take a few moments to consider, "What if I'd never met this person? How would my life be different?" Then, record all the ways your world is better because of them.

In the space provided, call to mind someone you care about. After considering what would happen if you'd never met, jot down some alternate life scenarios, and then list the ways they enhance your life. Throughout the week, repeat this activity with different people. BONUS: Pat yourself on the back if you can choose a person who you don't consider a friend. Write down what you've learned because of them.

Journal Space

Day/Date: _____

Weekly Tracker

Day/Date: _____

Day/Date: _____

Day/Date: _____

Day/Date: _____

Day/Date: _____

Day/Date: _____

Weekly Wrap-Up

Use this space to note any final observations about this activity. What surprised you? What was challenging? What did you like or dislike about the activity? Write your summary below.

_____
_____
_____
_____
_____
_____
_____
_____
_____
_____
_____
_____
_____
_____
_____

Well-Being Weekly Check-In
How are you feeling today? (Circle one)

Become an Emotional Alchemist
Transforming the Negative into the Positive

Feelings are never really good or bad...they just are. It's how we process them and act on emotions that make the difference as to whether or not they served us well. Consider a "negative" emotion that you've felt recently that caused you to feel unsettled in some way (e.g., anger, shame, etc.) This week, explore ways in which to use that emotion in a positive way. For example, if you are angry about a news story where someone was treated unjustly, could you...give to a charity that supports equality? Use it as a teaching moment with your kids? Each day this week, either work with the same emotion or choose a different one. Find creative ways to turn it into a positive experience.

In the space provided, write down your chosen "negative" emotion, recounting a recent or memorable event that caused it. In revisiting that event, consider how you would have made that event a positive one if it happened today. Or, if you're working with a present situation, brainstorm options for using your mental alchemy to transform this emotion into something positive.

Journal Space

Day/Date: _____

Weekly Tracker

Day/Date: _____

Day/Date: _____

Day/Date: _____

Day/Date: _____

Day/Date: _____

Day/Date: _____

Weekly Wrap-Up

Use this space to note any final observations about this activity. What surprised you? What was challenging? What did you like or dislike about the activity? Write your summary below.

_____
_____
_____
_____
_____
_____
_____
_____
_____
_____
_____
_____
_____
_____
_____
_____

Well-Being Weekly Check-In
How are you feeling today? (Circle one)

Spreading the Joy
Making Others Feel Valued and Appreciated

Throughout the day, we encounter strangers and people we barely know. In the popular book, **How Full is Your Bucket?**, the authors discuss every encounter being a chance to take a drop from someone's happiness bucket (e.g., a negative comment) or fill someone's bucket (e.g., a kind word or act of kindness). This week, seek out ways to "add a drop" to everyone's bucket you meet. This could simply be a "hello," a smile, or finding ways to sprinkle a little positivity around everyone you meet.

In the space provided, make a list of all the ways you sent out positive energy and added drops to the life buckets of those around you. Throughout the week, make a note of new events each day.

Journal Space

Day/Date: _____

Weekly Tracker

Day/Date: _____

Day/Date: _____

Day/Date: _____

Day/Date: _____

Day/Date: _____

Day/Date: _____

Weekly Wrap-Up

Use this space to note any final observations about this activity. What surprised you? What was challenging? What did you like or dislike about the activity? Write your summary below.

_____
_____
_____
_____
_____
_____
_____
_____
_____
_____
_____
_____
_____
_____

Well-Being Weekly Check-In
How are you feeling today? (Circle one)

"I Am Not My Thoughts."
Observing Without Judgment

Depending on who you talk to, we have an estimated 60,000 thoughts per day, most of which are negative and repetitive. Thoughts generate feelings that affect our mood and actions. Observing our thoughts as if we were on the outside of our minds looking in, allows us to remember, "I am not my thought. I am simply having a thought." Once aware of it, you can choose a newer, more positive thought, as needed. This week, set aside time to sit in a quiet space for at least ten minutes a day (20-30 minutes is ideal). As you close your eyes, draw awareness to your breathing. Notice what thoughts surface over time. Then, imagine they've turned into clouds. Allow them to float by and return your awareness to your breath. When you are finished, note what you observed.

In the space provided, list what thoughts surfaced. Did you notice any themes or patterns of thoughts? Were they positive or negative? How did the thoughts make you feel, emotionally and physically? If you noticed a negative thought, try writing down an alternate thought to "try on" next time you become aware of it. Throughout the week, document observations from your daily practice.

Journal Space

Day/Date: _____

Weekly Tracker

Day/Date: _____

Day/Date: _____

Day/Date: _____

Day/Date: _____

Day/Date: _____

Day/Date: _____

Weekly Wrap-Up

Use this space to note any final observations about this activity. What surprised you? What was challenging? What did you like or dislike about the activity? Write your summary below.

_____
_____
_____
_____
_____
_____
_____
_____
_____
_____
_____
_____
_____
_____
_____

Well-Being Weekly Check-In
How are you feeling today? (Circle one)

Creating Your Personal Symbol
Every Superhero Has One!

There is a reason why people wear symbols that represent their beliefs or as talismans or to set intentions…symbols are powerful. They remind us of our values and how we want to show ourselves to the world. If you had a personal symbol, what would it be? For example, if you wanted a symbol that made you feel protected, confident, and strong, what would it look like? What if you wanted one that demonstrated loving-kindness and compassion for the world? This may take some practice. Throughout the week, experiment with drawing variations of your personal symbol or just reflecting on it daily. Don't worry about whether or not it's a "good" drawing, nor try to explain its meaning to others. It only has to make sense to you.

In the space provided, let the doodling commence! Consider the purpose of your symbol, and then try drawing variations of it, or sketching in pencil so you can erase it and make changes. It doesn't have to be perfect, nor final.

Creative Space
The Week of: _____

Well-Being Weekly Check-In
How are you feeling today? (Circle one)

My Award
Waking Up to Your Greatness

Imagine you are on stage or at a private gathering with people who love and respect you. You are receiving an award for your contribution to the world, a cause, or for a personal achievement. Let your imagination run wild. What award did you receive, and why?

In the space provided, draw what this award looks like (i.e. Is it a small statue, a plaque? Something else?) Next, for the remainder of the week, review your award and "feel" as if you'd actually won it.

Creative Space

The Week of: _____

Well-Being Weekly Check-In
How are you feeling today? (Circle one)

The Path Not Taken
Being Mentally Flexible

Being mentally flexible means being able to adapt to change without becoming overwhelmed. Flexible thinkers are happier, less stressed, and more resilient. One way to develop flexibility is by trying something different, whether it is exploring a new nature trail, cooking a recipe you've never tried before, learning something new, or simply switching up your routine. This week, the challenge is to try one new activity each day.

In the space below, recall a recent situation where you were forced to be flexible. Maybe it was adapting to a delay at the airport, being stuck in traffic, or changing social plans. Whatever the situation, write down what happened, how you adapted, and the result. What did you learn from the experience? Next, try something new every day for the remainder of the week.

Journal Space

Day/Date: _____

Weekly Tracker

Day/Date: _____

Day/Date: _____

Day/Date: _____

Day/Date: _____

Day/Date: _____

Day/Date: _____

Weekly Wrap-Up

Use this space to note any final observations about this activity. What surprised you? What was challenging? What did you like or dislike about the activity? Write your summary below.

_____

_____

_____

_____

_____

_____

_____

_____

_____

_____

_____

_____

_____

_____

Well-Being Weekly Check-In
How are you feeling today? (Circle one)

Digging Into Your Strengths
Using Your Inner Reserve of Wisdom

We all face challenging situations. Sometimes, we doubt our ability to handle them. This week, when you encounter a stressor, recall a time when you've gone through something similar. Note how you overcame it and remind yourself, "I've been through this before and I can do it again." If it's a new event, take some time to write down all of the options for tackling this challenge, consider possible obstacles, and develop a game plan.

In the space below, write down your current stressor. What makes it stressful? If you've navigated something like this before, add a note about how you handled it. How will you manage this new stress? Anytime you face a challenge throughout the week or need to make a decision, draw upon earlier wisdom and experience for the answers. Make a note of what did and didn't work in the past.

Journal Space

Day/Date: _____

Weekly Tracker

Day/Date: _____

Day/Date: _____

Day/Date: _____

Day/Date: _____

Day/Date: _____

Day/Date: _____

Weekly Wrap-Up

Use this space to note any final observations about this activity. What surprised you? What was challenging? What did you like or dislike about the activity? Write your summary below.

Well-Being Weekly Check-In
How are you feeling today? (Circle one)

Intuitive Eating
Loving Foods That Love You Back

What you eat can impact how you feel, both physically and emotionally. And while sometimes a "comfort food" can support short-term feelings of security and contentment, some might not be the best for long-term health and well-being. This week's activity asks you to jot down what you eat and drink each day, and note how you feel within fifteen minutes of eating: Good? Bad? Neutral? For example, you may notice you feel a little lighter and happier eating a piece of citrus fruit, or maybe a little sluggish after eating a heavily processed fast-food meal.

Work in reverse! This week, keep track of what you eat each day. Then, on the last day, journal any observations. Are there foods that you've noticed may not agree with you? (e.g., itchy skin or something you never noticed before?) Any that gave you noticeably more sustained energy?

My Menu

MONDAY

TUESDAY

WEDNESDAY

THURSDAY

FRIDAY

SATURDAY

SUNDAY

Weekly Wrap-Up

Use this space to note any final observations about this activity. What surprised you? What was challenging? What did you like or dislike about the activity? Write your summary below.

_____

_____

_____

_____

_____

_____

_____

_____

_____

_____

_____

_____

_____

_____

Well-Being Weekly Check-In
How are you feeling today? (Circle one)

"This is a Disaster!"
Changing Catastrophic Thinking with Humor

There are, obviously, catastrophic events that happen in life that cause us trauma and grief. This activity, however, is NOT about legitimate disasters, but those times when everything seems to be going wrong, we're stressed out, and it's just "one thing after another." We may say to ourselves: "This is a disaster!" "This is awful!" Or, "I can't stand it!" This week, we'll be exploring situations and exaggerating them as much as we possibly can, to the point of it becoming ludicrous and even funny. For example, perhaps your angry boss who yelled at you in a meeting turns into a giant, fire-breathing dragon and burns the office to the ground, except for your desk. So, you still have to finish your work day. This is just one example, of course. By the end of the week, you might be saying to yourself, "It wasn't a disaster. In reality, it was just inconvenient."

In the space provided, consider a "disastrous" incident from your recent past (e.g., a missed plane, an embarrassing situation, etc.). AVOID picking something that causes significant pain or trauma (such as death or extreme injury). Choose something from daily life. Write down your disaster catchphrase (e.g., "I can't take it anymore!"), and then describe the incident in as catastrophic a way as possible using humor. Throughout the week, when you encounter minor upsets, rewrite the story with humor.

Journal Space

The Week of: _____

Weekly Stories:

Use this space to add additonal stories throughout the week.

Well-Being Weekly Check-In

How are you feeling today? (Circle one)

Forest Bathing & More
Finding Peace in Nature

Nature has always been a great healer. It reduces stress, enhances our immune systems, and makes us happier, healthier, and more resilient. This week, attempt to spend at least one hour per day in a natural setting. It could be immersing yourself in the forest and taking in all the sights, sounds, and smells around you. It might be sitting by the ocean, breathing in the salty sea air, and feeling the wind in your hair. Or, maybe it's visiting a local park and finding a quiet park bench to sit and gently observe your surroundings.

In the space provided, write everything you observed during your first day in nature, using all of your senses. Alternatively, sketch the landscape or even draw an element of nature (e.g., a tree or flower) during your experience. Throughout the week, seek out as much time in nature as you can commit to, and document your experiences at the week's end.

Creative Space
Day/Date: _____

Weekly Observations

Use this space to add additonal stories throughout the week.

Well-Being Weekly Check-In
How are you feeling today? (Circle one)

Draw Your Superhero Uniform
What is Your World Mission?

Maybe you're on a mission to spread love and compassion throughout the world. Perhaps you can heal the sick. What if you could fly? How would you use that power to change the world in a positive way? Or, maybe you are an artist who wants to inspire the world through art and music.

In the space provided, draw your superhero uniform. If you have colored pencils, pastels, crayons, etc., color your uniform in. What colors represent you? What shapes and styles? This week, as you observe the world around you, make a note of times when you would don your superhero outfit to help the world. (Who said personal growth couldn't be fun?)

 **Creative Space**
Day/Date: _____

Weekly Tracker

Day/Date: _____

Day/Date: _____

Day/Date: _____

Day/Date: _____

Day/Date: _____

Day/Date: _____

Well-Being Weekly Check-In
How are you feeling today? (Circle one)

Becoming a RAK-tivist
Random Acts of Kindness

In studies where people were asked to do something nice for themselves, or do something for someone else, people who chose to perform a random act of kindness or do a favor for someone else were reportedly happier than those who focused on themselves. This week, see how many random acts of kindness you can "rack up" in a day (at least up to 3). Whether it's letting someone in your lane while in traffic, opening the door for a stranger who is struggling, or checking in on someone who you perceive to be lonely, kindness matters.

In the space provided, list all the ways you can think of offering kindness to those around you (pets, plants, and the environment count, too!). Get creative so that you have a working list to draw from throughout the week.

Journal Space

Day/Date: _____

Weekly Tracker

Day/Date: _____

Day/Date: _____

Day/Date: _____

Day/Date: _____

Day/Date: _____

Day/Date: _____

Weekly Wrap-Up

Use this space to note any final observations about this activity. What surprised you? What was challenging? What did you like or dislike about the activity? Write your summary below.

Well-Being Weekly Check-In
How are you feeling today? (Circle one)

Noticing the Good
Learned Optimism

Optimistic people are typically healthier, live longer, enjoy better relationships, and are generally happier than those who focus on the negative. Interestingly, when we seek out the good things in life, our brains actually start scanning the world for more positive events, and we begin to "rewire" negative thought patterns with healthier and happier ones.

In the space provided, list all the positive events you've noticed so far today. They can be as simple as noticing a pet doing something that makes you smile to witnessing a random act of kindness. Nothing is too big or too small.

Journal Space

Day/Date: _____

Weekly Tracker

Day/Date: _____

Day/Date: _____

Day/Date: _____

Day/Date: _____

Day/Date: _____

Day/Date: _____

Weekly Wrap-Up

Use this space to note any final observations about this activity. What surprised you? What was challenging? What did you like or dislike about the activity? Write your summary below.

_____

_____

_____

_____

_____

_____

_____

_____

_____

_____

_____

_____

_____

_____

Well-Being Weekly Check-In
How are you feeling today? (Circle one)

Discovering Your Values
How Does Your World Change When You "Live" Your Values?

What are your values in life? Understanding what motivates you can help shape your purpose and define what is meaningful to you. Sometimes, when we find ourselves in a stressful situation or at odds with another person, it is because we have discovered something that doesn't align with our values. Clarifying your values can help you mitigate stress and prioritize that which is most important to you. Choose a value that is important to you. You'll likely have several, but pick the one that stands out at this moment:

Success   Adventure   Authenticity   Community   Wisdom
Beauty   Teamwork   Curiosity   Friendship   Gratitude
Courage   Creativity   Safety   Forgiveness   Wealth
Fairness   Family   Spirituality   Nurturing   Loyalty
Freedom   Honesty   Partnership   Kindness   Learning
Harmony   Humor   Joy   Love   Trust   Other_____

In the space provided, write about what this value means to you. How does it show up in your life? What do you do to use this value regularly? How do you feel when others do not share the same value?

Journal Space

Day/Date: _____

Weekly Tracker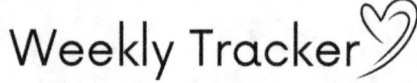

Day/Date: _____

Day/Date: _____

Day/Date: _____

Day/Date: _____

Day/Date: _____

Day/Date: _____

Weekly Wrap-Up

Use this space to note any final observations about this activity. What surprised you? What was challenging? What did you like or dislike about the activity? Write your summary below.

_____

_____

_____

_____

_____

_____

_____

_____

_____

_____

_____

_____

_____

Well-Being Weekly Check-In
How are you feeling today? (Circle one)

Problem-Solving Strategies
What's Your Solution?

Many people have their own problem-solving strategies that they implement in different ways depending on the circumstance. For example, one person might face a problem by writing down all the possible solutions, weighing the pros and cons of each, and making a decision. Another person might "go with their gut" and seek evidence to support their intuition for or against something. This activity is an exploration of understanding your current problem-solving strategy. [Hint: In future activities, you'll be asked to try a few different techniques.]

In the space provided, recall a recent situation where you were presented with a problem, personal or professional. Write down the problem, the steps you took to solve it, and what the outcome was. Note your problem-solving strategies throughout the week, and document them in the weekly tracker.

Journal Space

Day/Date: _____

Weekly Tracker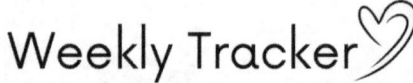

Day/Date: _____

Day/Date: _____

Day/Date: _____

Day/Date: _____

Day/Date: _____

Day/Date: _____

Weekly Wrap-Up

Use this space to note any final observations about this activity. What surprised you? What was challenging? What did you like or dislike about the activity? Write your summary below.

_____

_____

_____

_____

_____

_____

_____

_____

_____

_____

_____

_____

_____

_____

Well-Being Weekly Check-In
How are you feeling today? (Circle one)

Impossible Solutions
Trying Something Different

In a previous activity, you were asked to identify your main problem-solving strategy and simply observe how you solve problems, on a daily basis, throughout the week. This week, the challenge is to consider solutions from a completely different perspective. In this thought experiment, you are identifying the impossible, wacky, and creative solutions that couldn't possibly work. You might even pick your favorite comedy character and write how they would solve a problem. For example, what if the solution to being hungry was not to grab an apple from the apple cart but train a pet elephant how to retrieve it for you? The goal is NOT to act on these solutions but expand your thinking and become more open to creative solutions.

In the space provided, recall a recent situation where you were presented with a problem, personal or professional. Write down the problem, explore all the unpredictable and odd options, and make a decision. Then, imagine that it worked. Write down the fictional result.

Journal Space

Day/Date: _____

Well-Being Weekly Check-In
How are you feeling today? (Circle one)

Going With Your Gut
Exploring Intuitive Problem-Solving

Our bodies give us lots of physical clues for tapping into how we feel emotionally. Oftentimes when something goes wrong in someone's life, the person will say, "I should have trusted my gut." This activity is learning to tap into what your body is telling you and then seeking evidence to support and understand it. For example, if you are offered a job opportunity that seems perfect for you, but you feel a tightness in your jaw or sourness in your belly, explore what it might mean. Is it simply fear of the unknown or fear of failure, or is it not the right career move for you?

In the space provided, recall a current situation where you are presented with a decision to make. As you think about it, take a moment to close your eyes and tune into your body. Notice how you feel...first physically and then emotionally. Are those feelings good or bad? Write the problem and your "gut" response to it, and then seek out evidence to support how you feel. You don't have to necessarily make your decision based on these feelings...just observe.

Journal Space

Day/Date: _____

Weekly Tracker

Day/Date: _____

Day/Date: _____

Day/Date: _____

Day/Date: _____

Day/Date: _____

Day/Date: _____

Weekly Wrap-Up

Use this space to note any final observations about this activity. What surprised you? What was challenging? What did you like or dislike about the activity? Write your summary below.

_____
_____
_____
_____
_____
_____
_____
_____
_____
_____
_____
_____
_____
_____
_____

Well-Being Weekly Check-In
How are you feeling today? (Circle one)

Finding the Value
Reframing and Discovering the Lesson

We've all been there...that mortifying event that might have left us angry, embarrassed, fearful, insecure, or a combination of feelings. It might be that one event we ruminate on over and over again. This week, write down your perception of the event and the people involved. Next, choose to create an alternate version of that event or jot down the lessons learned. For example, if you forgot your line during the beginning of a speech, forcing you to pause and then start again, it may have felt embarrassing. You were certain everyone was either laughing at you or feeling sorry for you. During the instant replay, consider an alternative. For example, what if no one noticed you began again and thought you were repeating yourself for emphasis? What if the person needing to hear it most arrived late and it was good for you to begin again? Or, maybe the next speaker was fearful about their presentation and felt more relaxed when they saw how you overcame that hiccup with such ease.

In the space provided, write or sketch the event. Consider an alternative story or lesson, and jot them down in the remaining space. Throughout the week, any time you notice a "hiccup" in life, reconsider how you think people are responding and look for the lessons.

Creative Space

Day/Date: _____

Weekly Tracker

Day/Date: _____

Day/Date: _____

Day/Date: _____

Day/Date: _____

Day/Date: _____

Day/Date: _____

Weekly Wrap-Up

Use this space to note any final observations about this activity. What surprised you? What was challenging? What did you like or dislike about the activity? Write your summary below.

_____
_____
_____
_____
_____
_____
_____
_____
_____
_____
_____
_____
_____
_____
_____

Well-Being Weekly Check-In

How are you feeling today? (Circle one)

Gifts to the World
Your Three Gifts

"No man [or woman] is an island." We thrive when we are connected to others, particularly when we can receive support and ask for help when needed, and also give back to the world in a meaningful way. Social responsibility is an important aspect of personal power because it asks us to selflessly give of ourselves even though it is in the interest of the community versus a person's self-interest. When reflecting on your strengths and skills, what are three gifts that you give to the world? For example, do you give the gift of time by volunteering for a cause that you care about? Or perhaps you're the one family members turn to when they need a "voice of reason" to listen to all sides of a dispute and be the mediator? Or maybe you're the one to organize social events in your neighborhood and bring people together.

In the space provided, identify what your three gifts of the world might be. If you don't currently offer these gifts to society, how might you do so in the future?

Journal Space

Day/Date: _____

_____

_____

_____

_____

_____

_____

_____

_____

_____

_____

_____

_____

_____

_____

_____

_____

_____

_____

Weekly Tracker

Day/Date: _____

Day/Date: _____

Day/Date: _____

Day/Date: _____

Day/Date: _____

Day/Date: _____

Weekly Wrap-Up

Use this space to note any final observations about this activity. What surprised you? What was challenging? What did you like or dislike about the activity? Write your summary below.

Well-Being Weekly Check-In
How are you feeling today? (Circle one)

Discovering a Power Animal
Calling on Your Inner Reserves

Many ancient spiritual practices include the belief in power animals, whereby a practitioner might have one animal that they call on regularly for support. Even if you don't share that belief, for this exercise, choose an animal (real or mythical) that either embodies how you would like to feel or provides the support you need. For example, perhaps you want to imagine that your power animal is a tiger that reminds you to be assertive and strong in meetings, or maybe it's a songbird that reminds you to be optimistic and keep singing.

In the space provided, draw your power animal. Consider the characteristics of this animal. You might even research more about its lifestyle habits to make more of a connection. Throughout the week, you'll be looking for ways in which your power animal can support you. Jot down what you discover.

Day/Date: _____

Weekly Tracker

Day/Date: _____

Day/Date: _____

Day/Date: _____

Day/Date: _____

Day/Date: _____

Day/Date: _____

Weekly Wrap-Up

Use this space to note any final observations about this activity. What surprised you? What was challenging? What did you like or dislike about the activity? Write your summary below.

_____
_____
_____
_____
_____
_____
_____
_____
_____
_____
_____
_____
_____
_____
_____

Well-Being Weekly Check-In
How are you feeling today? (Circle one)

Walking Meditation
Mindful Awareness

Studies suggest that people are up to 60% more creative when they take brisk walks. Physical activity is also associated with better health outcomes, including less anxiety and feelings of stress. There are many ways to approach a walking meditation. For this activity, the pace is completely up to you. You might walk as slowly as possible and become immersed in your surroundings, noticing everything around you with all of your senses (e.g., the birds singing, the smell of orange blossoms, etc.). Or, if you are moving quickly, notice your breath as you inhale and exhale, notice the feel of your feet walking on a dirt path, or the weight of your legs as you climb an incline.

Try to go on your mindful walk for at least 20-30 minutes. After you return, drink water if you need to. Then, write about everything you observed either within your surroundings or your body itself. If you discovered that you ended up with your mind wandering, that's okay. Jot down what you observed and try to be more mindful as you repeat this activity throughout the week.

Journal Space

Day/Date: _____

_____
_____
_____
_____
_____
_____
_____
_____
_____
_____
_____
_____
_____
_____
_____
_____
_____

Weekly Tracker

Day/Date: _____

Day/Date: _____

Day/Date: _____

Day/Date: _____

Day/Date: _____

Day/Date: _____

Weekly Wrap-Up

Use this space to note any final observations about this activity. What surprised you? What was challenging? What did you like or dislike about the activity? Write your summary below.

_____
_____
_____
_____
_____
_____
_____
_____
_____
_____
_____
_____
_____
_____
_____

Well-Being Weekly Check-In
How are you feeling today? (Circle one)

Telling a Different Story
What Else Might Be True?

Most people have experienced a situation where they were certain that their interpretation of an event was true and accurate, when in reality, something completely different was going on. For example, if someone frowns at another person, the recipient might assume the frowner was angry with them, maybe didn't even like them. When, in reality, perhaps the person suffered an injury and was in pain. Or, what about someone not showing up for an event? One might assume they forgot, they got lost, they changed their mind about going, or something happened to them on the way. This is an exercise in challenging what we think we know, and asking ourselves, "What else might be true?"

In the space provided, write down an experience you had recently that involved another person. What was happening? What beliefs did you have around the event? Next, ask yourself, "What else might be true?" Jot down some alternate options that may be contrary to what you first thought.

Journal Space

Day/Date: _____

Weekly Tracker

Day/Date: _____

Day/Date: _____

Day/Date: _____

Day/Date: _____

Day/Date: _____

Day/Date: _____

Weekly Wrap-Up

Use this space to note any final observations about this activity. What surprised you? What was challenging? What did you like or dislike about the activity? Write your summary below.

_____

_____

_____

_____

_____

_____

_____

_____

_____

_____

_____

_____

_____

_____

_____

Well-Being Weekly Check-In
How are you feeling today? (Circle one)

Super Powers and Kryptonite
Know Thyself

While developing healthy self-esteem is important, another extremely important part of self-awareness and acceptance is Self-Regard. Self-Regard is a component of emotional intelligence and requires us to accurately examine both our strengths and weaknesses and maintain that self-confidence and self-acceptance, despite imperfections. It also requires that we give equal attention to the good and bad without it diminishing our sense of self or exaggerating only our strengths. This week, take some time to examine both.

Reflect on the questions, "What are my top 3 strengths?" and "What are 3 areas in my life where I'd like to see improvement?" Write your answers in the space provided. Over the week, take a moment each day to either utilize one of your strengths or sharpen an area where you'd like to improve.

Journal Space

Day/Date: _____

Weekly Tracker

Day/Date: _____

Day/Date: _____

Day/Date: _____

Day/Date: _____

Day/Date: _____

Day/Date: _____

Weekly Wrap-Up

Use this space to note any final observations about this activity. What surprised you? What was challenging? What did you like or dislike about the activity? Write your summary below.

_____
_____
_____
_____
_____
_____
_____
_____
_____
_____
_____
_____
_____
_____
_____
_____

Well-Being Weekly Check-In
How are you feeling today? (Circle one)

Giving Up Control
Letting Go of "They Must" and "I Must."

It would be nice if everything and everyone operated exactly as we think they should. Unfortunately, there is much in life that we can't control. And feeling that lack of control leads to stress. This week is an exercise in acceptance. This is not to suggest that we accept abuse or things that are dangerous to our physical and mental health. Instead, we are identifying the subtle times where we find our internal dialogue saying things such as, "In order to be happy, I must be able to___" [fill in the blank], and "They must do ___ [fill in the blank]." What happens when you let go of the "musts" for a day and choose to accept what is?

In the space provided, begin to notice when people don't "follow your rules." For example, maybe your significant other does something to annoy you (like loading the dishwasher differently from you), or a co-worker always leaves their desk (which is next to yours) a mess, when you prefer your surroundings to be neater. What happens when you relinquish control over all those little things? Write your observations below. Throughout the week, look for ways to be more accepting.

Journal Space

Day/Date: _____

Weekly Tracker

Day/Date: _____

Day/Date: _____

Day/Date: _____

Day/Date: _____

Day/Date: _____

Day/Date: _____

Weekly Wrap-Up

Use this space to note any final observations about this activity. What surprised you? What was challenging? What did you like or dislike about the activity? Write your summary below.

_____
_____
_____
_____
_____
_____
_____
_____
_____
_____
_____
_____
_____
_____

Well-Being Weekly Check-In
How are you feeling today? (Circle one)

"I Can Do It Myself!"
Learn When to Ask for Help and When to Be Independent

Growing up, we may have been raised in one of two camps. Camp #1 required that we ask permission for everything. Perhaps this was based on culture, religion, gender, or the family dynamic. Camp #2 subscribed to the "I don't need anyone" mindset, either because those in this group thought they had no one to turn to and had to go it alone, or perhaps they were taught that asking for help was a weakness. This week's activity asks you to take a look at how you operate most of the time, and how this may change based on circumstance. Are you decisive and yet know when to ask for support? Reflect on this below.

In the space provided, recall a time in the past when you relied heavily on other people's opinions to make a decision, possibly ignoring your feelings as unworthy. Next, recall a time when you took decisive action without asking for support. In both situations, identify what went well, and what didn't. For the remainder of the week, document times where you were independent or when you needed support.

Journal Space

Day/Date: _____

Weekly Tracker

Day/Date: _____

Day/Date: _____

Day/Date: _____

Day/Date: _____

Day/Date: _____

Day/Date: _____

Weekly Wrap-Up

Use this space to note any final observations about this activity. What surprised you? What was challenging? What did you like or dislike about the activity? Write your summary below.

_____
_____
_____
_____
_____
_____
_____
_____
_____
_____
_____
_____
_____
_____

Well-Being Weekly Check-In
How are you feeling today? (Circle one)

Time After Time
Maximizing Your Day

Sometimes, people get so caught up with the responsibilities of day-to-day life that they either rush through tasks, barely being present for them, or they miss out on participating in events or activities that have meaning. In this activity, reflect on how you spend your time on a regular basis, and how you would rather be spending your time. Notice which areas in your life are lacking that you would like to devote more attention toward. This can involve time at work, time with friends and family, time pursuing a hobby, focusing on spirituality or growth—whatever is important to you.

In the space provided, write down one area of your life that you wish you had more time to devote to. What makes it important to you? What would you do if you had more time? Over the course of the week, note how you focus on this area of your life and look for small ways to add it into your day-to-day or enhance your existing practices.

Journal Space

Day/Date: _____

Weekly Tracker

Day/Date: _____

Day/Date: _____

Day/Date: _____

Day/Date: _____

Day/Date: _____

Day/Date: _____

Weekly Wrap-Up

Use this space to note any final observations about this activity. What surprised you? What was challenging? What did you like or dislike about the activity? Write your summary below.

_____
_____
_____
_____
_____
_____
_____
_____
_____
_____
_____
_____
_____
_____

Well-Being Weekly Check-In
How are you feeling today? (Circle one)

To Know Me Is to Love Me
And Learn to Love "You," Warts and All

Building a healthy sense of self-regard is more than just "liking yourself" and building confidence. It is about accurately identifying your strengths and weaknesses without it changing your self-view. In other words, you are neither exaggerating your skills nor diminishing your value. Instead, you have a clear perception of yourself and can love and accept yourself without judgment. It also allows you to grow as you hone in on capitalizing on your skills and building potential areas of weakness into strengths.

In the space provided, answer these questions: 1) "What is my greatest strength?" (e.g., integrity, resourcefulness, etc.) 2) How has this strength served me over the years? 3) What is my greatest area of weakness? 4) How has it hindered me over the years? For the remainder of this week, you will have the opportunity to build on both your strengths and your weaknesses to serve you better.

Journal Space

Day/Date: _____

Weekly Tracker

Day/Date: _____

Day/Date: _____

Day/Date: _____

Day/Date: _____

Day/Date: _____

Day/Date: _____

Weekly Wrap-Up

Use this space to note any final observations about this activity. What surprised you? What was challenging? What did you like or dislike about the activity? Write your summary below.

_____
_____
_____
_____
_____
_____
_____
_____
_____
_____
_____
_____
_____
_____
_____

Well-Being Weekly Check-In
How are you feeling today? (Circle one)

A New Perspective
Developing Empathy and Forgiveness

Many arguments over religion, politics, world views, and values could be defused by 1) Pausing before reacting to what is being said and 2) Attempting to understand the other person's perspective. When we practice empathy, we also develop mental flexibility, deepen our relationships, learn impulse control and become more forgiving (both to ourselves and others), all of which contribute to building our resilience and personal power (not to mention making us more fun to be around!).

In the space provided, think of a minor altercation you've had with someone in the past, or consider a topic where a friend has the opposite view of a situation as you do. Write about the situation FROM THE OTHER PERSON'S PERSON'S PERSPECTIVE. You may not get it exactly right, but that's okay. This is just an exercise in perspective-taking.

SPECIAL RULE: No bad-mouthing the other person. (e.g., writing, "I think this way because I'm a terrible person!")

Journal Space

Day/Date: _____

Weekly Tracker

Day/Date: _____

Day/Date: _____

Day/Date: _____

Day/Date: _____

Day/Date: _____

Day/Date: _____

Weekly Wrap-Up

Use this space to note any final observations about this activity. What surprised you? What was challenging? What did you like or dislike about the activity? Write your summary below.

_____
_____
_____
_____
_____
_____
_____
_____
_____
_____
_____
_____
_____
_____

Well-Being Weekly Check-In
How are you feeling today? (Circle one)

Silencing the Inner Critic
Challenging Your Internal Voice

Each of us has an inner critic. It's that subconscious voice that tells us we're not good enough, smart enough, or whatever-enough. It's been there so long, that we may not even notice how prevalent its presence is. The first step toward silencing the inner critic is to become aware of when those negative thoughts surface. Only then can we begin to gently challenge those unhelpful thoughts and begin to replace them with supportive thoughts, ones that better serve us.

In the space provided, list or write about some of the negative self-talk that goes on in your head. If you're not yet aware of what that might be, consider a situation or situations recently where you felt "less than." (i.e., where you felt you lacked the skill or talent to accomplish something. What did you say to yourself about that event?)

Journal Space

Day/Date: _____

Weekly Tracker

Day/Date: _____

Day/Date: _____

Day/Date: _____

Day/Date: _____

Day/Date: _____

Day/Date: _____

Weekly Wrap-Up

Use this space to note any final observations about this activity. What surprised you? What was challenging? What did you like or dislike about the activity? Write your summary below.

_____
_____
_____
_____
_____
_____
_____
_____
_____
_____
_____
_____
_____
_____
_____
_____

Well-Being Weekly Check-In
How are you feeling today? (Circle one)

Passive, Aggressive...Just Right
Assertive but Kind

There's a fine balance between being passive when we would rather voice our concerns, or aggressive when we are forcing our opinions as "facts." Right in the middle is being able to be fully present and assertive, while not diminishing anyone else's power. It involves building kindness around assertiveness. This week's activity encourages us to notice when we behave in passive, aggressive, or assertive ways in an honest assessment of our behavior. If we typically find ourselves falling on one end of the spectrum or other (i.e., overly passive or overly aggressive), this is an opportunity to fine-tune our approach.

In the space provided, document one example of a time when 1) you were passive in a way that was not helpful to you, 2) a time when you were overly aggressive, and 3) a time when you were perfectly assertive while practicing kindness. Over the course of the week, look for daily ways in which you can walk the balance in your interactions with the people around you.

Journal Space

Day/Date: _____

Weekly Tracker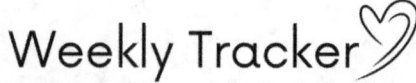

Day/Date: _____

Day/Date: _____

Day/Date: _____

Day/Date: _____

Day/Date: _____

Day/Date: _____

Weekly Wrap-Up

Use this space to note any final observations about this activity. What surprised you? What was challenging? What did you like or dislike about the activity? Write your summary below.

_____

_____

_____

_____

_____

_____

_____

_____

_____

_____

_____

_____

_____

_____

Well-Being Weekly Check-In
How are you feeling today? (Circle one)

Right Now, Later...Never
Looking Before You Leap

There are some who say "yes" to every situation only to regret it later, leaping before looking to see if "yes" is the best response. Others might respond angrily to an idea that offends them, spilling out words they wish they could take back. And, at the opposite extreme, there are those who may feel unable to commit to a situation or speak up for themselves, until they have all the facts...which never happens, leading to no movement whatsoever. This activity asks you to consider how you react to situations. Do you "shoot from the hip" and respond quickly, or do you weigh your options and choose your words carefully?

In the space provided, write down a recent personal or professional event that you responded to. Note whether you felt your response was impulsive, just the right balance, or lacked follow-through. What, if anything, would you do differently if presented with a similar situation in the future? For the remainder of the week, note your response style as situations arise.

Journal Space

Day/Date: _____

Weekly Tracker

Day/Date: _____

Day/Date: _____

Day/Date: _____

Day/Date: _____

Day/Date: _____

Day/Date: _____

Weekly Wrap-Up

Use this space to note any final observations about this activity. What surprised you? What was challenging? What did you like or dislike about the activity? Write your summary below.

_____

_____

_____

_____

_____

_____

_____

_____

_____

_____

_____

_____

_____

_____

_____

Well-Being Weekly Check-In
How are you feeling today? (Circle one)

What's Your Vision Statement?
What Do You Bring to the World?

Many companies have a vision statement that explains who they are and what they plan for the future. Individuals can also write a vision statement in order to help clarify their view of the world and their part in it. Vision statements can be related to work or a personal way of being. For example, one vision statement might read, "I bring joy to the world with my positive attitude and nonjudgmental support." Or, "I support men and women seeking to make significant changes in their lives by providing resources to help them grow." This week's activity is to hone in on your vision. Since we are such multifaceted beings, this is not an easy task. Therefore, you may end up revising your vision throughout the week. At the end, decide which one, or combination of them, makes the most sense for you. Print it up and post it somewhere where you can re-read it daily.

In the space provided, try writing out a few vision statements. If it's helpful, first jot down words that embody who you are and your purpose (e.g., help, support, encouragement, create, love, etc.). Throughout the week, repeat your vision and revise as needed.

Journal Space

The Week of: _____

Well-Being Weekly Check-In
How are you feeling today? (Circle one)

3 Wishes Come True
The Genie in a Lamp

Imagine a genie offers you three wishes. In this scenario, the world is already at peace, and everyone on the planet has food, shelter, and access to resources that ensure their needs are met. There's no wishing for more wishes, so choose wisely! You go to sleep at night and when you awaken, these three wishes have come true. What did you wish for?

In the space below, write, draw, create a collage or in some way illustrate what you wished for. Over the next week, take a moment each day to come up with three new wishes and record them in the space provided. The sky's the limit! (Or, is it?)

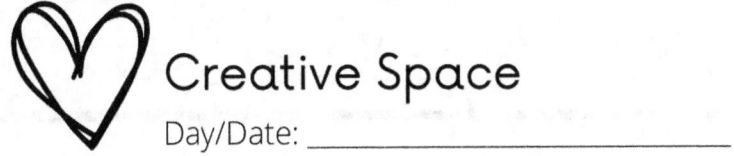

Creative Space

Day/Date: _____

Weekly Tracker

Day/Date: _____

Day/Date: _____

Day/Date: _____

Day/Date: _____

Day/Date: _____

Day/Date: _____

Weekly Wrap-Up

Use this space to note any final observations about this activity. What surprised you? What was challenging? What did you like or dislike about the activity? Write your summary below.

_____
_____
_____
_____
_____
_____
_____
_____
_____
_____
_____
_____
_____
_____

Well-Being Weekly Check-In
How are you feeling today? (Circle one)

"My Future's So Bright."
Stepping Into Success

"Success" means different things to different people. For some, it's a certain level of financial power, rising through the corporate world, or being famous. For others, it might be being well-respected in their community for their nonprofit work or raising a family. No one interpretation of success is better than another. The problem is when our vision of success clashes with others' expectations, or we begin to doubt our vision and compare ourselves with someone else's vision of success.

Take a few minutes to ask yourself, "What does success mean to me?" In the space below, write down what it means to you to be successful and how successful you are feeling at this moment. How are you feeling about your current life's journey and what are your success plans for the future? Over the next week, each day, note something you've done that day to contribute to your vision of success.

Weekly Wrap-Up

Use this space to note any final observations about this activity. What surprised you? What was challenging? What did you like or dislike about the activity? Write your summary below.

_____
_____
_____
_____
_____
_____
_____
_____
_____
_____
_____
_____
_____
_____
_____

Well-Being Weekly Check-In
How are you feeling today? (Circle one)

"My Future's So Bright."
Stepping Into Success

"Success" means different things to different people. For some, it's a certain level of financial power, rising through the corporate world, or being famous. For others, it might be being well-respected in their community for their nonprofit work or raising a family. No one interpretation of success is better than another. The problem is when our vision of success clashes with others' expectations, or we begin to doubt our vision and compare ourselves with someone else's vision of success.

Take a few minutes to ask yourself, "What does success mean to me?" In the space below, write down what it means to you to be successful and how successful you are feeling at this moment. How are you feeling about your current life's journey and what are your success plans for the future? Over the next week, each day, note something you've done that day to contribute to your vision of success.

Journal Space

Day/Date: _____

Weekly Tracker

Day/Date: _____

Day/Date: _____

Day/Date: _____

Day/Date: _____

Day/Date: _____

Day/Date: _____

Weekly Wrap-Up

Use this space to note any final observations about this activity. What surprised you? What was challenging? What did you like or dislike about the activity? Write your summary below.

Well-Being Weekly Check-In
How are you feeling today? (Circle one)

Go Forth and Be Musical!
Dance, Sing, Play…

Listening or playing music that we enjoy releases "feel-good" hormones in our brains and promotes greater well-being, better memory, more creativity, and better overall health. But unless we're musicians or performers, we might be listening to music while doing other things such as working, exercising, or driving. This week, take a few "music breaks" to either simply listen, play (if you play an instrument), sing along, or move to the music. The goal is to bring music to the forefront and notice which songs uplift our moods the most.

In the space provided, either write down songs that bring you joy throughout the week, sketch or create a collage describing how music transforms you.

Creative Space

Day/Date: _____

Well-Being Weekly Check-In
How are you feeling today? (Circle one)

Freestyle #1
Choose Your Own Activity

Name of Activity:

In the space provided, write, sketch or create a collage representing your weekly activity of choice.

Creative Space
Day/Date: _____

Weekly Tracker

Day/Date: _____

Day/Date: _____

Day/Date: _____

Day/Date: _____

Day/Date: _____

Day/Date: _____

Weekly Wrap-Up

Use this space to note any final observations about this activity. What surprised you? What was challenging? What did you like or dislike about the activity? Write your summary below.

_____
_____
_____
_____
_____
_____
_____
_____
_____
_____
_____
_____
_____
_____

Well-Being weekly Check-In

How are you feeling today? (Circle one)

Freestyle #2
Choose Your Own Activity

Name of Activity:

In the space provided, write, sketch or create a collage representing your weekly activity of choice.

Weekly Wrap-Up

Use this space to note any final observations about this activity. What surprised you? What was challenging? What did you like or dislike about the activity? Write your summary below.

_____
_____
_____
_____
_____
_____
_____
_____
_____
_____
_____
_____
_____
_____
_____

Well-Being weekly Check-In
How are you feeling today? (Circle one)

Freestyle #2
Choose Your Own Activity

Name of Activity:

In the space provided, write, sketch or create a collage representing your weekly activity of choice.

Day/Date: _____

Weekly Tracker

Day/Date: _____

Day/Date: _____

Day/Date: _____

Day/Date: _____

Day/Date: _____

Day/Date: _____

Weekly Wrap-Up

Use this space to note any final observations about this activity. What surprised you? What was challenging? What did you like or dislike about the activity? Write your summary below.

_____
_____
_____
_____
_____
_____
_____
_____
_____
_____
_____
_____
_____
_____

www.ingramcontent.com/pod-product-compliance
Lightning Source LLC
Chambersburg PA
CBHW081616100526
44590CB00021B/3468